Dark Chocolate & Peppermint Tea:
Warmth for the Fireside

Courtney,

It's been a pleasure getting to know you. Thanks for all the laughs & help. You're going to be a great social worker.

-Heather

Dark Chocolate & Peppermint Tea:
Warmth for the Fireside

Poetry by
Huda Bint Adnan

Illustrations by
Jolene Sadoun

<u>Dedication</u>

To the moon of my life, Hina.
Though you hang in the calming dark skies, I
can still feel your presence close to me.
When you unveil your beauty to the world, you
are starkly illuminating and remarkably
effervescent.
Thank you for being my limbs when mine lost
their control.
I know that my words have always been too
many and too loud for you, but here I am again
with words that I have said too many times and
have meant with too much heart—without an
ounce of regret.
Here is a lifetime of love—a collection of words,
both voiced and silenced.
Here is a lifetime of feelings, transcending all
bounds to find words, when you cannot, to find
hope, when you cannot, and to find love, when
you cannot.
Thank you for everything.

Huda Bint Adnan

Hands out, forever
reaching towards you,
but you *always* run away,
abandoning my
outstretched palms.
You are the line
of life,
embedded in my skin,
one that stretches
far and wide,
retelling the
stories of where
I have been.
Do not let go.
You are written
in my palms.
You are the
present,
future,
and all that
has gone.
I will
reach out
towards you,
always.

"always"

Huda Bint Adnan

When you are drowning in an ocean of burdens, I will swallow some of the sea, so you can regain the balance that you have always sought out in me. Though my lungs may burn with salt, and my heart may burn to ashes, I will return to your shore, with every single wave that crashes. The sand will settle in my stomach and you will learn to float, for I am already an ocean and you were destined to be a boat. Let not your body sink, let not your soul drown. Let your heart wander, until you want it to be found.

Huda Bint Adnan

This is for
the lonely nights
and the heavy hearts,
the bereft arms
and the aching wants.

This is for your
maddening sanity
and your disheartened reality.
This is for your burdened shoulders
and your frail bones.

This is for those
who believe that they
cannot go on.
You can.

Huda Bint Adnan

Disclaimer:
There are two things that usually run away from me: my
thoughts & my imagination.
Please bear in mind that these pieces are not meant to be
taken in a literal manner.

Huda Bint Adnan

<u>Acknowledgements</u>

Niha: You have always been truthful, honest, caring, encouraging, and wonderful in all ways. Thank you for looking at my work so carefully and meticulously with welcoming eyes and a warm heart.

Sahifah: It is quite remarkable how you are able to be brutally honest and equally encouraging at the same time. I very much appreciate how you have always generously lent me your wisdom and affectionate guidance.

Nour: Certainly, I am grateful for your continuous encouragements, reassurances, and straightforwardness. You have never ceased to praise my work and it has truly helped me build my confidence. Thank you.

Wajiha: Your enthusiasm for my writing has been a source of courage. Thank you for photographing inanimate objects for an outstanding book cover. Without a doubt, you've been my amazing cheerleader.

Jolene: The pages of this book have become richer by your pen. Thank you for tolerating my type-A personality, for putting up with my incessant deadlines, and for producing illustrations that have exceeded all expectations.

Mohammad: This book wouldn't be what it is without your last minute additions. Thank you for your help, friendship, and for writing a gracious biography.

Naveed: Thank you for all your patience, your advice, and your continuous support—all through the astonishing world of the internet.

Thank you all for easing my doubts, listening to my worries, and always giving me your thoughtful advice. I am honored to have had all of you be a part of this process—it has been a dream come true. Thank you.

Huda Bint Adnan

Contents

Huda Bint Adnan

Womanhood

Pricked and plucked,
poised with perfection,
pulled and plundered,
no aid and no protection.
Pampered with prettiness,
and polluted with lies,
these are the grievances,
I can no longer hide.
Peppered with petals
of lost hopes and dreams,
these are the women
who have been loosened
at the seams.
Pedestals have pushed
our prides to the floor,
for our wants are already written,
and we cannot ask for more.
Seldom do we speak
of such sacred sorrows,
for you listen to us today,
only to silence us tomorrow.
Practice what you preach,
pay heed to the poor.
We do not just speak for ourselves—
of that, we are sure.

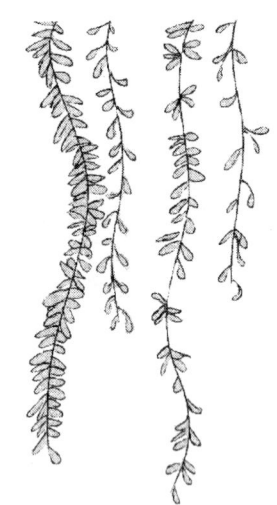

// "we are women; we are the world"

You envy
my edges
and curves.
Take it.
Take my
skin and
take my
bones——
make them
your home.
Take too,
the marks
of self-hatred,
nights loathing
the skin I
was born in.
Take the hips
and the lips,
take my waist,
and my face——
take it,
the full package.
Take the voice
too.
It told me I was
not good enough,
but maybe, it won't
do the same to you.

// "you envy what you do not know"

Blood drips between my thighs,
I rise with anger and pain on my tongue and belly,
wondering how to get rid of the terror that is building up
inside of me.
I cry with hopelessness, trying to cope with the idea that I will
suffer throughout eternity with these cramps.
Dark chocolate and peppermint tea, I'll sit next to this fire
until I've become a warm sea of heat and desire,
so watch me turn these untamed tides ashore,
first I'll bleed and then I'll be no more.

// "these are the burdens that women bear"

I am learning to build these walls back up again because I swear I thought I wouldn't fall, but here I am picking myself up from my knees and dusting off all the lies from my sleeves. I'm putting my heart back where it belongs, inside of my chest where it will come to no harm. Do not come back with apologies, do not fall to your knees for I cannot lend you any more sympathy. Take your lies, take your hate, and should these ties sever, I can assure you that it was only fate. I am ready to get past this and I am ready to move on. I want to find myself with the right, for I've been with the wrong for too long.

// "my heart has been in the wrong hands for too long"

Two lights
shone into the
hearts of my
parents, when
I was born,
yet the world
shuns me into
darkness,
because I must
bear the
punishments
of womanhood.
My womb
will be
brightened
with great light,
but your
ignorance
will always
bask you
in darkness.

// "women are light in a world of darkness"

I've spent years
staring at the wall
wondering if I'd ever
get through it all.
I've spent years
staring out the window
wondering if any
fruits would emerge
from the seeds that
I have sowed.
I've spent years
looking at the reflection
hoping that each time
I did not flinch at my
own complexion.
I've spent years
sitting fixedly,
wondering if I
could ever live
up to my destiny.

// "will i achieve greatness?"

Outstretched palms,
empty and wanting.
A haunting past weighs
heavy my grieving heart.
Lips parched and burning—
yearning for quenching silence.

// "sadness is a loyal friend of mine"

Some days are not good days. Isolation is the best consolation when tremulous trepidation is the only sensation one begins to feel. Leave me alone on wintry days where I no longer know what I'm doing. Let me wander within the expanse of my own mind and find the thoughts that are always brewing. I am only human—I feel lonely in my own skin. I don't know how to go on or how to even begin. How do you crawl out of your body and start anew? There is no vessel for my soul, no other body I can sew. Undo my seams and let me be free. I doubt I'll ever even amount to the person I want to be.

// "blue is the color of my heart"

I am like the plants
I watered—
dry, aching—
waiting for life
in this dying world—
hoping to grow roots
in a soil that I have
never belonged to.

// "i left my roots back home"

Lungs bloom
with flowery breaths
and petals of
whispers caress my
neck. Vines
tangle themselves
around my waist,
only they are your
arms locking me in
an embrace.
A bed of leaves
tickle my toes
as I walk along
roses, planted in rows.
Featherweight tulips
crown my head, and
in this strange world,
daffodils are red.
A meadow of wonder,
growth, and sunlight,
envelop me in a
life of dazzling
light.

// "a flowery world that exists only in my mind"

My birthday wish list stretches to the moon and back, but I guess you could say that my number one wish is to get you back. Give me a pocketknife so I can slash my wrists in the bathroom and hide the scars when you come home too soon. Give me a handgun so I can kill the demons that haunt me. I'll pull the trigger as I look in the mirror not realizing the demon I've been trying to get rid of was always inside of me. Give me a typewriter so when the ink that stains my fingers is not enough to calm me down, I can pick up that vintage piece and smash it against the wall watching the keyboard pieces fly to the ground in poetic motion. Give me a bottle of sleeping pills so I can chase that bad dreams of the night away, because even when you haunt me with nightmares in the day, at least you actually stay and give me company. I get lost within my mind—I get lost drowning in my grief for things that have come to pass and things that have not come at all. Forgive me, for liking blood more than ink. Forgive me for being an anchor—my only destiny is to sink.

// "birthday blues"

I was an old house
haunted by your ghost.
The stain of your
kisses on my swollen
lips would not disappear.
I ached to be new,
to be built
again from the dirt.
I ached to be strong
enough to fill my rooms
with people who belonged.
My rooms have long
been empty.
I have crumbled
beneath the
harsh years.
I have been
forgotten.

// "i shouldn't have let you live inside of my heart"

It took me years to
accept myself—it took
me ages to realize that
another woman's beauty
does not subtract
from my own, and
if I believed that it did,
I would never be able
to find a home
in my own bones.

// "you are your own home"

Gentle tremors and
stirring wake my soul
and as goose bumps rise
on my skin, I am
filled with longing.
I ache for tranquil sleep
and dreams that don't
turn into nightmares.
When will my heart
stop burning with
emptiness?

// "empty hearts lead to empty thoughts"

Women have sacrificed
everything, yet we do not
glorify their identity
by naming them
warriors.
Is only
sacrificing bodies
worth a title?

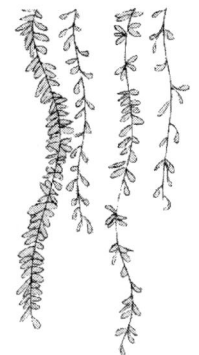

// "we sacrifice our lives for a world that has never honored
us"

Stained panties—bloodied red,
I wish I hadn't even gotten out of bed.
I just try to remember what my mother once said,
quoting our book of religion and peace,
"Verily with every hardship comes ease, and you will find
God in places beyond what your eyes can see."
Caught in between wanting to throw up,
and wanting to eat,
each wave of pain has got me beat.
I feel a spasm of agony run through my veins,
burning my core,
from my head to my toes.
I cry for relief from these cramps—
from this stamp of womanhood.
With every drop of blood
that escapes me,
I pray that babies with smiles
brighter than their father's
await me.

// "god rewards the patient and the righteous"

How quickly
we hope to
forget the men
and the scars
they left on
our skins—
how much
will we
scratch our
flesh to bleed
out the venom
of a love
that was never
pure—never
destined.

// "bleeding out your poison"

These hands have done it all. They've memorized your face and the crevices of my own body—they've built up bridges and they've torn down walls. They've had bruised knuckles, cuts and burns, but these are the same hands that have allowed me to learn. I can point to your smile, my finger along your lips, tracing the way your hands slide down to my hips. I can point to my wrist, where I've cut too many slits, a phase that I've grown out of. The scars show now, darker than my skin, but I know now, that life can begin again.

// "my hands are still filthy from my past mistakes"

Blood pearls
adorned my
throat.
You had
choked me
with your love
as the monster
inside of me
woke.
I was thirsty
for blood.
I was thirsty
for revenge,
hell-bent on
getting a
noose
wrapped around
your neck—
just as you
had bejeweled
me with
your love.

// "love is deadly"

I remember when I used to stay up until 2 am so I could shower and wash away my sins of the night. As the blood swirled around in the drain, I wondered why you had become the bane of my existence—why you couldn't just let me live without your breath on my neck. I wondered why you always stained my skin with your black kisses. I wondered why your fingerprints left filth all over my white soul and why I wasn't bold enough to put an end to your existence. I wonder why I wasn't bold enough to put an end to mine....

// "i can still see the stains of your fingerprints on my heart"

As a woman, I have been taught to bend for men who only seek shelter under my branches—not a nest or a home. I have bent many branches and have broken many bones, but as an ancient tree who has always bent—whose limbs have been cut off, I can grow no more. Hurricanes have torn me in half, tornadoes have ripped me from my roots, but it was you, oh it was *you,* darling man, who had cut my beautiful branches in two with your bare brutish hands. The winter stripped me of my blooms, and left me cold in the dark, but it was you, *it was you,* who tore apart my heart. From then on, my leaves never grew, the flowers never bloomed, and never again will I find a home for my shredded roots.

// "i am not a temporary stay"

Heaviness grows
in my heart and soul
and I am breaking
from weighty burdens.
My bones are fragile
and they are beginning
to crack
and crumble
and I am
falling
into
darkness again.

// "darkness is lovely"

Do I not
bleed new life?
Do I not
give birth
to my blood?
Am I only
beautiful
when adorned
naked on a man?
Am I not
gorgeous
when I
am bejeweled
with
beautiful life?

// "god put life inside of women"

Silent, solemn sacrifices slip and stumble off your skin as we
sit side by side.
Stardust settles on her slumbering statue and we stare in
sadness, sagging with sober suffering.
Swollen, salty sickness surges through our starry-eyed stares.
Such is the senselessness that we must succumb to.
Sadistic savages suck on every salacious desire that we have.
Sparkling suffocation surrounds our souls.
Simmering and sensual sins swarm our sanguine selves,
sticking to our skin, to our cells.
Stab your sword into our sturdy stance.
We are women who will only die with strong-willed defiance.

// "we are made of stardust and strength"

I tried settling down in my bones, attempted to make them a lasting home, but my meddling thoughts weighed me down like drowning stones. I asked myself how I would survive, how I could even think that I'd come out alive, but a voice in the depths of my mind told me that I had the strength. I didn't know what lengths I'd have to take, but for God's sake I knew that I had to try. I spent days crying, staring out the windows through blurred vision, struck by the constant collision of heavy heartbeats against my ribs and a mind full of dizzying thoughts that would not give in. I shouldered your pains and worried my soul to death, but I swear that if I could take back all the hurt, I would give you my very last breath. I swear I wanted to let you hold the world in your palms, but I'm afraid that I was selfish and I wanted the world to stay in my own arms. I wreaked havoc in your life and I bewitched you with my swaying hips and I wish to God that I could wipe away my taste off of your drying lips. I don't want to come running back—never would I dream of coming back to you, but I have finally put my heart to peace and that's all I could ever hope to do.

// "there is always a war inside of me"

A half-eaten plate,
a used napkin—
I was no longer pure.
These are the words
my mother used
to describe my
mistakes.
Who would eat
from an eaten plate?
Who would use
a dirty napkin?
I was only destined
to be used.

// "used"

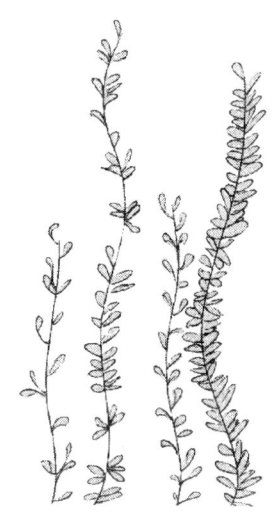

My lips have
forgotten
how to stretch
into curving lines
of joy,
from which galaxies
exploded and
flowers blossomed
into vivid
memories.
I can no longer
remember
what eyes that
have not cried
feel like.
I can't recall
a time when
my skin didn't
recoil away
from bones
that betrayed
themselves
for you.
I always
gave myself up,
for you.

// "i lost myself"

I shudder to think how many times I handed myself over to someone in just a blink of an eye—how I didn't even think twice because I'd give everything including the kitchen sink. The truth is that I loved too much and I loved too hard, and that is precisely how my heart has scarred, and has been battered—shattered to pieces by broken promises of "I love you." I've managed to glue together the pieces, but like a white sheet of paper that's been crumpled, I have too many creases to straighten out. I sought to find shelter in so many hearts, but humans aren't medicine and sadness isn't art. I found shelter in God's love and His grace, because who else would bother to look down on my face despite my sins, and despite my mistakes—who could mend this disease, this tiring heartache? God is good, He is truly great. Not once did He fail to free me of this weight—this burden of truth that breaks my back—this purity and goodness, there's so much that I lack. A tear-streaked face, a melting heart, I may not be a saint, but this sure is a good start. Perhaps the beginning of a journey so beautifully pure, in which I might find, this disease's cure. A lack of piety, humility and so much more, I have grown tired of keeping a score. The sins pile high, reaching the sky, my good deeds are few, and I have yet to pay my dues. God, help me get better, help me get well. I promise to try but only time will tell. Grant me goodness at every turn, there is so much to see, so much to learn. Give me strength and opportunity, give me peace and tranquility. If you are pleased with me on Judgment Day, surely I know I have possessed well, my dignity.

// "god answers our silent pleas"

I always had trouble
knowing when
a man was
being friendly,
or when he was
being a pervert.
I was taught to
quietly avert my
gaze should it ever
meet with someone
who only ever saw
me as meat
to be slaughtered.

// "what is a world without such fear?"

Sinful slumber satiates our sickly sweet surrenders.
Thoughtful threnodies throw tantrums like thunder.
Arched angles made from my arms above your aching head.
Soulful stars sing of sorrowful sinners after scarlet sunsets.

// "this is how we love"

He colored her chest
black and blue like the sky,
painted it red, like morning sunlight,
flushed her skin purple,
like the milky way galaxy,
and then ran his fingers over her,
white lies and apologies.
Every morning she rose,
pink with blushed cheeks,
forgiving him for the pain,
and for giving her such love,
that made her so weak.

// "he does not love you if he hurts you"

Adam's apple
has been stuck
in his throat
until this very day,
but no one asks
about the secrets
that Eve has choked
upon, since the
beginning of time.
She always knew
man would fall,
but never knew
that he would
also be a
woman's downfall.

// "for pious men & women, their home is Paradise"

What other secrets
does my house hide?
Does the carpet stain
scream of my
impurity?
Does the door hinge
still cry from the
time he slammed
it open with his foot
because he was
too busy holding
me in his arms?
Will my bed speak
against me,
hating to be the
one catching me
when he threw me

onto it?
Does the wall
crumble with
repulsion,
remembering
how I was pushed
back into it,
my spine
rubbing off
her sins?
If these walls
could speak,
what truths
will they spill?

// "will these walls be a witness against me?"

Screams resonate, trapped in the depths of my mind. I bleed onto pages—writing, hoping, praying that they will be silenced.

// "this is why i write"

I'm a beauty with flaws,
I'm a beauty with cracks,
I'm a beauty that is scarred,
but I've got a bone in my back,
that keeps me strong,
and keeps me tall.
I'm a beauty that's indestructible,
and I'm not afraid to fall.
Truth is I'm a beauty,
not in arrogance or vanity,
but the fact that I have survived,
my own mind's insanity.

// "my mind can be cruel"

Flourishing fantasies flower into faces,
stardust settles in between spaces,
tender touches tethered to your throat,
such are the sighs that softly, she spoke.

// "i fantasize about love"

My bones have been ripped apart like roots from the ground and when these gaping cuts were poisoned, I unleashed no sound. Quietly, I contemplated in which state I would like to be found. Curled in a ball of sadness and guilt, or standing on a throne of bones that I woefully built.

// "i will not stay broken"

Silence weighs down my ivory bones, I cannot carry this heavy burden solely on my own. The flowers in my lungs have begun to wilt and the usual balance that is in my life is now beginning to tilt. My ribs are breaking—I can already see the cracks. My heart is turning to ebony, spreading to darken the wings on my back. Who am I, what have I become? What do I call this drowning feeling and where has it come from? Brighten my soul and lighten this weight. Help me become good again, before it is too late.

// "a plea"

I cannot apologize
for the slashing
of my tongue or
the harshness
of my mouth,
or how my
words rain and
pour or how
they abandon
you to droughts.
I will not succumb
to the prim and
proper ways of
ladies who are
quiet slaves,
just as I cannot
let you men dictate
from inside your
ancient caves.
I have recovered my
worth, wit, and ways,
and I shall not
let you arrange
my God-given
fate.

// "god gave women life & men seek to take it away"

Fire

Wood creaks
in empty hallways,
ghostly whispers
of loneliness
slither on the walls.
Cobwebs grow in
corners, and dust
settles in every
crevice of my
heart.
Confined in my
own body,
lost in my
mind,
this empty
vessel,
I cannot leave
behind.
It waits for her
angel to
come back in
control,
for it was
this very
angel to
whom she had
sold her
soul.
Forced to
wander and
drift

until the end of time—
for when
Lucifer
walks the
earth, I will
no longer be
confined.

// "the devil lives inside
of me"

P.S. I still burn from where your fingers touched my skin——a mark of passion and a mark of sin, but I will never let you win.

// "to the devil that lived inside of him"

I.   Reminisce, remember this—we used to be so good at all of this. That was a time of bliss, a time when our ribs kissed each other, getting caught up and tangled in bones, and we all hoped to God that we wouldn't end up alone. I ache to hear the phone ring just one more time, so that I can hear your voice and pretend that everything is fine. It's not fine, when has it ever been? I mean this is just another war that I'll never win. Battles have torn us apart and there is so much pressure choking my heart that I don't even know where to start.

II.   Healing—the thought of recovering makes me reel with pain. All these efforts will be in vain—like praying for a drought in this pouring rain—why would anyone pray for a drought? You've slammed my head in a pool of water, and I was a fool to think that you wouldn't slaughter a lamb like me. You are a lion needing to hunt and I was too close to the flames—I should have known that in the end I would only get burnt.

// "i have tasted fire"

I want your fingers to burn from where you touched me. I want your eyes to burn for all that they have seen. I want your lips to burn from what they have tasted. And I want your heart to burn with all the love you didn't really mean. I want you to burn relentlessly, just as I had burned for you. And I want you to remember that from the ashes, you can start life anew. But first you must burn—let your flesh become dust and only then will you know what becomes of such blistering lust.

// "we will burn together"

I dream of fiery constellations erupting in my palms, but they burn my fingers and when I try to lick away the heat of the flames, my tongue falls out with heavy sadness. I am aching for sleep where I don't wake up screaming into the darkness of night—where my eyes don't burn with the branded silhouette of your face—where my gums don't bleed from tasting your name in my cavernous mouth. I captured colors of ebony and indigo on the insides of my elbows where my flesh always remembers your violent touch and the bruises don't fade away so quickly. My soul is wounded from being lonesome in its shell. I yearn for another's light to radiate into my heart so maybe the darkness can lift and the restlessness can finally slip away.

// "my lonely soul needs light"

Blood and fire in my mouth, blood and fire on my tongue, blood and fire in my eyes, blood and fire in my lungs. Will my burning heart ever stop bleeding?

// "this fire bleeds"

There is a flame that flutters freely in all of us, but we have burned candle wicks for the infernos that have died too soon, and when fires set ablaze our souls, there was hardly enough room to breathe. We either blow out our livelihood or give it too much fuel. Kindle your flame so that it flutters and dances, do not let it waste away in vain.

// "cherish the fire inside of you; some have lost it altogether"

Can you see the guilt in the circles under my eyes? Can you see the relief? Can you see how heavy my heart was, filled with lies? Can you? Can you see the fire that I once possessed—how it's been blown out? Can't you see the freedom I have been given, no longer weighed down by doubts? I am free. Let me be.

// "i will find my flame again"

I am not special, or exceptionally unique. I am flawed and broken in more places than one. My bones are ivory and my blood is crimson and my skin teeters towards color rather than paleness. My eyes are brown that tinge hazel in the sun. My lips are swollen in the mornings from dreams of your kisses and bites. I love too much and give too little when I should be generous, and give too much when I should be miserly. I have a heart that beats, each time with the permission of my Lord. I have wounds that bleed, when they are not freed from my constant picking and pestering. I have scars of unhappiness on my wrists, but those dark times have now turned to bliss. I have an uncontrollable tongue that speaks of uncontrollable desires. And I have this spark of passion in my heart that seems to turn into fire, when I'm around you. It flickers and burns, blackening the edges of my pure white soul, and I don't feel the void in there, because around you, I'm whole. But when you are gone, and I can think, I skid to the hazardous brink of loneliness and sadness, for I am human and I've made far too many mistakes, all for the sake of pleasure. I am human. I am human. I am human. Please forgive me.

// "your lips tasted like hell"

Rekindle my flame,
it had burnt out too soon.
Fuel this inferno,
like the scorching sun
in June.
Reignite the fire,
let it burn up
all the embers,
for this is a fire that
we must
always remember.

// "remember your fire"

He was like an unfinished sentence, an incomplete story, a window half open, a door half closed, a king's heart at the end of a sharp sword—a halfway glory. He was like the perfect blue skies—soft and sunny rays, but with cool breezes flowing through your hair. He was like a breath half-taken, an almost kiss—the kind of moment you regret even years after wondering what went amiss. He was like the space between two lovers when there should have been none. He was the kind of man you wanted to run to and run from. He was burnt orange and burgundy leaves swirling in the autumn wind and falling off trees. He was the pause in a monologue that quietly fades away and he was the rhythm of a song that makes your hips sway. He was a halfway stanza, an incomplete verse. He was the angry pressure in my head, right before he burst. He was the flame of a fire, orange and blue. I get lost in the flickering heat of his fluctuating hues. He was a million pieces of complex magic and I swear if you knew how much my heart is pulled towards him, you would think it's tragic. He's like a half-drunk glass of water, easing the parched ache in your throat. He's like the tight knot you choke upon, at the end of the rope. He's the gap in between lovers, sentences, and words—but he is the wind beneath my wings, and I am his ever-soaring bird.

// "half—"

Raspberry juice stains my fingers and you slip them in between your lips, stealing sweetness off of the tips. Pink juice paints your teeth and you grin at me with a mouth full of sin. Roots sprout from your palms and bloom into flowers of blood-red like the sky at dawn. Your laughter echoes off the walls, as you pull me on top of cluttered, granite countertops. And I melt, like warm butter dripping off of toasted bread and I don't know whether I'm hungry for your lips or your skin, but I take whatever I get as you pull me in.

The river of juice turns into blood and it runs its course, slithering over the curves of my skin and it flows, red red red. Your eyes have become dark, black like the night and hell glows from their depths, flicking its tongue like a snake, hungry for prey. I fall into the pits, burning my flesh as I desperately flail to hold onto something. I find nothing, only shards of glass that plunge into my veins and I bleed, unknowingly offering myself as a sacrifice for your raging inferno.

// "you were not an angel"

My father never knew of my sins, never knew that there was a devil inside of me trying to win me over—trying to govern my mind. It spent years poisoning my veins with a venom so harmful, it would end up burning my brain. I would douse it in fire and fuel it until it was black with ash, but I could never leave my mistakes in the past. The fire burned my insides, turning it to soot and dust, but I knew that I had to try to stop—I knew that I must. I failed. When fire slipped out from my tongue and burned my lips too, I could not fathom how I did not realize that the devil was always you.

// "the devil follows me everywhere"

I have been a
gaping wound,
bleeding
and ghastly.
I have been
sprinkled with
salt,
and burned
with fire.
I have been
dug deeper
into—
but I always
regain
my shape.
I will always
recover.
I will
be born
again.
I will
be born
anew.

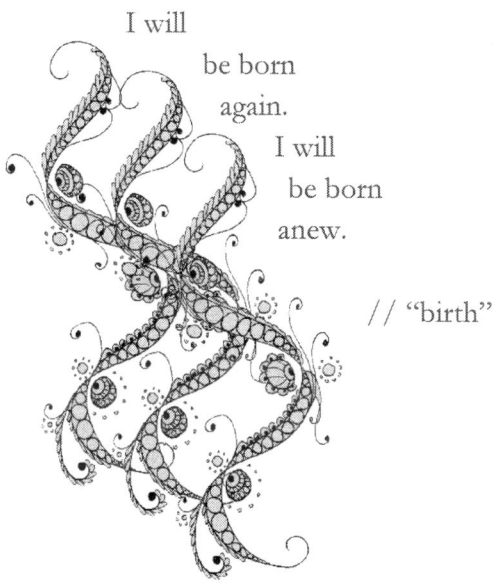

// "birth"

"Fire or flames, it's all the same, it burns my tongue just the same, it burns my heart just the same. My words are fire and they cannot be tamed."

// "i am made of fire"

I want to burn my skin, watch the flames lick the flesh until I am nothing. I want to rise up in fumes, casting dancing shadows across your face, as I shed darkness throughout the room. I want your eyes to burn, just like mine do when I look back on sinful memories. I want your flesh to burn, just like mine does when it remembers your skin and your lips and your tongue. I want your mouth to burn, just like mine does when your name slips out from between my teeth and I bleed my gums dry. This is a wickedness I cannot easily shed and I am aching to be born anew.

// "burn with me"

Shattered, battered, craters in my chest that have left me in tatters. A fragmented soul—remnants of memories and dreams, open for the world to see when you pulled at my loosening seams. I guess nothing is what it seems. A bright beam of light radiated from your heart to mine, but it was not passion, it was a hazardous fire that ignited my perilous desires. "The girl on fire" collapsed in blazing flames, never to rise or return again.

// "the girl on fire"

You've tainted my blood and set my heart on fire, I am continuously chanting your name with nothing but desire and I should be ashamed, but I cannot stand up from my kneeling state and I refuse to do so until my hunger is satiated. This burden of love and want is weighing down my back, and I am beginning to lose the willpower that I already lack. Come back, you heartless fool, please come back.

// "this love burns my flesh"

Toxic fumes burn plumes in my lungs and I can't breathe anything but scorching fire as my insides turn into ashes. Flashes of the past burn hot behind my eyes, binding them closed with imprints of what has already passed. My vision is branded with your blackened face and your burned eyes, red and black, hot with desire and hate. Fate had washed its hands of your lies but it didn't wash its hands of you and I, so here we are stuck on these coals as our skin melts into puddles, folding into each other like candle wax. There is no looking back, there is no turning back, and there is no going back.

// "your love feels like hot coals"

Will our tongues
collide with
fiery madness?
Will we light up
the world with
our love?
Will only the insides
of our mouths
blaze in bright
flames?

// "let's set this world on fire"

The last time we met, your greedy, lacerated lips kissed my fingers and as I looked at your hungry eyes, your mouth bleeding into my palms, I swear that I wanted to cut my fingers off. I wanted to burn away your touch hoping that spilling my own blood would somehow purify me of my sins and of your filthy hands. I can still feel your fingers in my sleep, slithering up my skin, tightening around my throat— ready to drag me down to meet that demon that was always inside of you.

// "i can't tell the difference between you and the devil"

I am mystified, mortified at your presence deep within my essence. I sense your condescending smile and your petrifying glare, and I dare not turn my head to meet your sultry stare. You are the sun, blazing and scorching on my back, and you are the moon, silent and cold, upon my chest. I cannot rest knowing that your gaze is upon my breast and I grow festered and pestered from your close proximity. It's too close for comfort but you didn't care that much for personal space anyway. You took shelter in my head at any time of day and I could not even say a word to make you go away. Stay, I pray you don't hear my heart's craving to slave for your every desire. I perspire, entirely undone by your passionate fire. I have been set ablaze and there is no waking up from this lovely daze.

// "a lovely blaze"

Self

When your back
curves and bends
beneath the
weights and
the burdens,
remember to face
eastwards,
for there is no
better direction
in which to
turn, and shatter
into pieces of
peaceful relief.

// "god will put you back together"

Exhaustion
penetrated
my body,
grabbing my ankles
and
dragging me down.
I looked to the sky
hoping to tear
away the canvas
and glide to the
Heavens.
I longed to
gaze upon
God's beauty.
The world's affairs
made me fatigued.
I longed to
be free.

// "death is true freedom"

On my knees I fell in the hopes that You would forgive me. I clasped my hands together, tears streaming down my face, begging Your Grace for His mercy. I gazed at the stars knowing that only the All-Merciful could answer my plea. My joints swelled with pain, but I did not shift from my knees. The gates of Heaven opened and You sent down a pouring rain. With the clap of thunder and a strike of lightning, I felt Your presence pierce my veins. My throat throbbed and my heart beat loudly in my chest. I was not filled with dread, but alas, a slight unrest. The torrent soaked my clothes and blinded my eyes, but the drops felt cool against my skin, just as they did when You first opened the skies. I parted my lips in the hopes that I could taste Your mercy on my tongue. I caught a few drops in my mouth, and I felt Your mercy fill my lungs. My God, so merciful, how could He not be, when He has graced our hearts with love and humility? I will only bow down to You, Oh Lord, I will only seek Your aid. For without Your guidance, we would only have gone astray.

// "i spoke with god"

India, how wicked were you to spit me out with such venom over oceans and seas? India, how could you hate your child so much that you exiled her so far away from your breast? India, do you not love me because my complexion is not milky and gold? Has it become too dark to fit your mold of standards? Am I just skinny limbs of worthlessness that you set me aside like trash? Was I too foreign to grab ahold of your hand? Did my skin remind you of that oppressive British man? Am I not your child? Am I not your blood? I ache for you more than my ancestors ever would.

// "i miss you mother india"

Revel in your rage,
you will never be the same.
Rise with your anger.

// "the devil's whispers"

I want to bloom
in the very roots
that tell me
I am a foreigner.
I want to plant
myself between the
trees of mango
and lychee
and between all those
who tell me that I am
not fair, nor lovely.
I want to reach for
the very sun that
beats down
on my back,
scorching my flesh,
burning it black.
I want to be one
with this land
that I call home.
I want to be one
with this land
that I ache
to call my own.

// "home"

I always considered myself to be the prettier sister, but I didn't realize that each day, with that thought in my mind, my head just got bigger. What good is a pretty face when you have an ugly heart? I felt sicker when I found that arrogance and pride had poisoned my veins with pitiful lies. Recognizing my pride was the start of a painfully honest journey. And I pitied myself because even with my wide hips and full, pink lips, my head was bigger than the earth's circumference and I gained no confidence with such knowledge. I failed to grasp human decency as I stared at my reflection in the mirror, getting sucked into this false perception that perfection could be achieved. A good heart makes any face shine with beauty and light, but my heart—oh what a hideous sight. It was black and hellish, filled with jealous envy and self-pity. I have drowned my mother's lungs with sadness and despair and continuously tried to convince her that I genuinely cared. I have never lived up to my sister's expectations, where I was actually innocent in comparison to others. Boys left burns on some inches of my skin and I could not find the power within me to stop such sins, to stop from such an addictive cycle of pleasure and regret. My heart, once white and pure, was ugly and black with no hope to be cured or to be saved. I was too scared to find God, too scared to ask for mercy, because after all, would even the Most-Merciful want to forgive me? Would He grant me shade on the fateful day if I came back to His way? Or would He turn me away to punish my transgressions? Would my sessions of confessions and crying grant me redemption? I cannot fathom the idea that the Fire awaits me simply because I fell into my deceptive desires.

// "arrogance is poisonous"

Ammi implores, "What is wrong,
why are you sad?"
But I cannot tell her about the
shame
that weighs me down
and the burdens of
having a tired soul,
and a heart filled with
envy and jealousy
for all it has lost
and for all that was
never mine.
How can I tell her
that my mind
buzzes with the
cruelest thoughts
when I am asleep?
And when I wake with
the taste of death
on my lips,
it is so sweet
and inviting.

// "my mistakes are too grave"

When your arms
are lonely,
and your veins
begin to lose blood,
I will flood
your soul
with compassion
and warmth,
so that you
may find
the strength
to go on.
When your heart
is heavy and
somber, filled
to the brim
with tears of
anger, I
will lift the
weight off
your shoulders,
so that you may
breathe.

// "i will love you when you cannot love yourself"

My nights
have been lonely,
and silent—
dreams begin
as calm and
collected,
only to become
shockingly violent.
I am being
strangled with
the American
flag, while the
Star-Spangled
Banner
plays grimly
upon my
death.
I feel the
word "freedom"
slip off my tongue
with my
last breath.

// "land of the free [white man]"

Free yourself of
worldly shackles.
You are bound
to no one
but God.
This vessel of flesh
was made purely
to worship.
Why do you
loathe your sacred
skin?

// "your home lies in paradise"

And sometimes I just want to lay in bed and never get up because I'd rather stay in this cocoon of oblivion than get up, get out of the house and face a life of utter despair, humility, and hatred. Such malice follows me in many forms. Most forms take the ugly, black shape of disappointment. But sometimes, it takes the form of the most innocent smiles and the simplest of gestures and those hurt the most.

// "this world will break your bones"

I have screamed
my lungs sore
in the darkest
of nights.
I have cried
my eyes dry
and almost
lost sight.
I have cut
my veins
open just
to bleed
them empty.
And the world
does wonder
why I have
given up
the will to fight.

// "life is tiresome"

If my existence was to fade,
each particle turned to dust,
and carried off in the waves,
would my essence give life to the earth,
or would it poison it with death?

// "am i made of stardust or poison?"

Unhinged self-destruction is the worst kind of demolition of the soul—the kind that makes one feel as if they are tripping over fiery coals and falling straight into a raging inferno of emotions that threaten to overthrow and spill out of every crevice known and unknown. I have sewn together pieces of myself countless times, but they always come undone and each thread has frayed beyond recognition. I am growing helpless and hopeless, wishing that I would break less just so I can feel like less of a mess. But I am spilling over, splattering and crashing into earth-shattering waves. I have always been too much.

// "too much"

Tea and thoughts of you,
Seaside mornings are lovely
Can tides drown my mind?

// "i want to drown in thoughts of you"

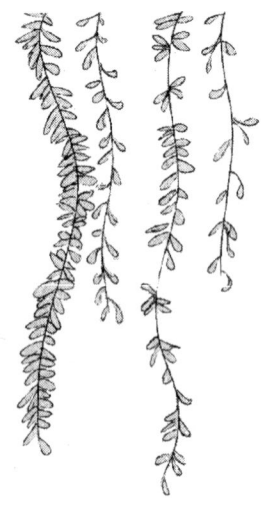

Men say their
"I love you's"
a little differently
than us women,
but always remember,
that they are capable
of voicing their
emotions with
tender kindness.

Find a man
who can massage
coconut oil
into your hair
and
weave
your locks into
a tight braid.

Find a man
whose eyes
glimmer with
love when you
come home
and he massages
your feet
and shampoos
your hair.

Find a man
who is a lover
at all times
of the night,
especially when
your dreams
are haunting
and lonely.

// "this is a love i hope to have"

She sprinkled stardust
on her pillow,
hoping to create a
universe in her
head, but her dreams
always faded when she
got out of bed. The
Milky Way dissolved into
the black holes of her
mind, and she
always swore to me
that her world was always
more important than mine.
How was I supposed to
know that I was
her world?
These are the sacrifices
of a mother.

// "my mother's world is full of sacrifices"

I refused to believe that I was composed of stardust, always chose to dust off my shoulders of the hopes and dreams that were too far-fetched to ever come to be. I never looked at myself in the mirror—wouldn't get caught gazing at all the flesh that formed my frame. I was always too afraid to see what flaws lay in between my shoulder blades. I never believed that nakedness was to be revered—I always feared my body. I was so good at hiding, but that was before I learned the art of smiling.

// "i can no longer fold myself into nonexistence"

Written in the blood
of our family's women
is the power and courage
to break hearts that were
never meant to be ours.
We bear the strength of
carrying burdens from
ourselves and the thousands
before us.
We will not cower beneath
the weight of men who have
never found in us, a home.
They have only come
for a temporary passion
that we have too much
dignity to offer.

// "our dignity means more than your fragility"

Resist and defy,
these lovely whispers of mine,
and you will survive.

// "the devil's whispers pt. ii"

Gaze into the inside
of your wrists,
where you will

 find veins
pulsing with life
in webs of
vibrant blue
and red
snaking underneath
your skin.
Listen close and
hear the hum
and thrum of
humanity
that buzzes
within.

// "there is goodness in our veins"

My spine curls—
fervent thoughts
creep along its length.
I am falling, slowly,
gracefully into
the depths of your
dark, haunting eyes.
Blood lines the
inside of your lips
but you look at me
with wanting and
with shaking passion.
Your nails are
dirty with filth
and ashes of bodies
you burned to dust.
I wonder if I
will meet the same
fate.
Suddenly, you smile
crookedly—sharp teeth
beckoning my skin
and my blood
to your inviting
tongue.

// "you are beautifully wicked"

Dear heart of mine,
make room for God,
like He's made room
for you.

// "we are immensely blessed but infinitely ungrateful"

I cannot resist as my own two fists beat against my chest in anger and agony, yelling at God, asking why He did this to me. Why He chose to breathe life into my soul, why He wrote for me to become this old and still be a disappointment. Why me, why me, why me? Oh Lord, am I amongst the saved or will punishment find me six feet under the dirt, in my grave? I ask you God, to give me life once again and give me the strength to uphold my name. Soften my heart to this beautiful Islam, Oh God, please give me the strength to uphold this Iman.

// "forgive me"

Things to Remember

I. God is there. You just need to call upon Him.

II. When God sends you the same test over and over and over again, do not weep with agony, pray for strength and pray for ease—God just wants to see you succeed.

III. Dark chocolate is medicine for an aching soul. So is prayer. Try both.

IV. Taste the salt of your tears, it tastes like humanity.

V. Wash your sins away with Wudhu and Istighfar. Forgive yourself so you can move forward. The past will stay in the past so long as you let it. It is not a comforting ghost, for ghosts do not comfort the living, they only haunt.

VI. Learn the words of God. You will be greatly enlightened.

VII. The Golden Rule: Love yourself.

VIII. Sadness isn't romantic. Feed your soul with even the smallest of happiness and watch it grow and blossom.

IX. Women should build each other up. Forgive your sisters, your mothers, your daughters. We come from great women who wouldn't want to see us bringing each other down.

X. Learn to let go. Your destiny was written by the Greatest of Writers. Leave your fate to Him—the Maker of all that exists.

// "be kind to everyone for some bear the burdens of Atlas"

Tragic treasures always fade.
What good is silver when
there is gold to be made?

// "our faces will age, but good hearts last forever"

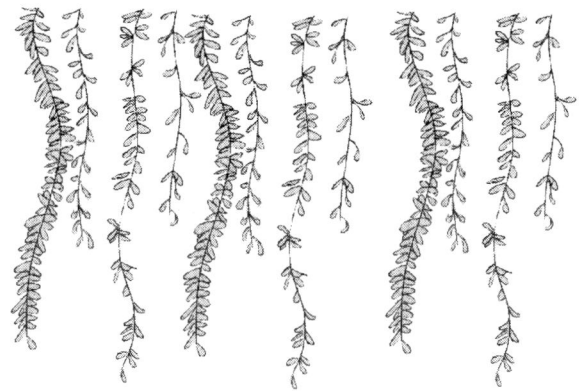

We grew with palms full of luxuries,
in a land that was not of our ancestors, but oceans away from
their graves.
Our parents swam the sea with empty pockets, hearts full of
hope, and heads full of determination.
They broke their backs to grant us spines and when we didn't
understand their stories of loss, we turned around to tell them
that they were spineless.
The poison of ingratitude ran through our veins—it filled our
lungs every time we breathed this wretched air, with the
stench of genocide and enslavement.
And we accused them of not understanding how trivial our
problems were. How could we know the pain of breaking our
bones solely
to build from those pieces, a life.

// "we were their lives"

These empty hands have given me nothing but shame—they have done nothing but carry out the same mistakes over and over again. These empty hands have held no fruits, have done no goodness, and have spread no love. These empty hands knead each other's palms in nervousness and anxiety as I think of all the harm they have caused for me. These empty hands have known no warmth. They have not felt another's in a very long time and it seems they may not know what another's skin feels like for a while. These empty hands miss you. These empty thoughts miss you. These empty arms miss you. I am empty without you.

// "empty hands and empty hearts"

I used to abhor
my language—
thought it
was distasteful
and rough,
simply because it was
not soft like silk,
or smooth like
the flow of
a river.
Each word was
like a wave
crashing into
the shore—
broken and

magnanimous,
but I realized
that I was
like those
waves—broken
and magnanimous,
and my voice
demanded to
be heard,
to break
barriers and
overthrow
the balance of
the earth.

// "my language is beautiful and so am i"

Do not tell me that distance is impossible. I have swam oceans and climbed mountains just to separate myself from him when hormones are present. I have repressed each screaming urge and silenced every aching cell just so I don't sell my soul to the devil of temptation—so I am not thrown into a land, where there is no salvation and no mercy, where all that is broken was once an element of fragility, and has shattered infinitesimally. Do not tell me that distance is all loss and no gain because despite the strain, I have refrained from losing. I have seen willpower and control rise, stronger than ever before with great glory and might, and distance does not mean a lost fight, but a victorious holy war and despite being gassed in an open air prison, I have found myself emerging, unbroken.

// "patience is a virtue"

Haunting echoes and
whispers of your lips
tracing my skin,
envelop me in
reminiscence
of so much bliss.
All the innocence sucked
away in a matter
of seconds, only because
you and I were not
satisfied with firsts,
so we had to have
seconds.

// "you were my bad habit"

Guide
not, only
our tongues,
but also
our hearts,
so our lungs
may be filled
with You,
and we breathe
only remembrance.

// "a prayer"

You are the
pressure building
in my brain,
the same pressure
that thickens
my veins,
trapping air
in its wake
and leaving me
gasping
in pain.
You will
blow me up,
exploding
with agony,
and ruptured
fragments will
only expand
into shards of
empty air.

// "you give me agony"

I've begun to say "I love you" again and I swear that for a while, I thought I could actually control my tongue but I can't and it slips out in between sentences because I love humans—I crave their company, but I abhor their savagery and so-called "humanity." And I swear that I stopped—at one point I really did, I bid my tongue to be silent even when I had no other choice but to respond, and I always held back, but I have so much to love to give—there is so much that I want to give back. I wish to tell you above this love that overflows my veins, how it drowns my lungs with warmth, how it drives me almost insane when I keep it bottled up, and when I bury it deep, it always comes back up, and it always begins to seep. It seeps throughout the crevices and the holes of my flesh, and out of my mouth it slips, right out of my constricted chest. I cannot keep it inside for long, no matter how much I try, this love is a love that erupts from my soul, and it'll rain and it'll pour, until every inch of me is dry.

// "i love too much"

Why do birds
chirp at midnight?
Do they call
to lovers who
have not yet
returned home?
Do they sing
in mourning
for lovers
lost and gone?
Do they not
know that darkness
is not for
cheerful merriment?
It is the
time that one
must learn
to accept
loss.

// "darkness is full of sadness"

For The Man Who God Has Written As Mine

Come closer, let us roam nowhere together. Let us smell the
dirt and become one with the earth. Let us get back in touch
with nature so that maybe we can finally attempt to be better.
Let us try this new venture. Let us climb trees and mountains,
swim in creeks, and drink from clear blue fountains. Let us
gaze at the stars in the sky and the stars that we find in each
other's eyes. Let us count the clouds that pass and count each other's scars when the heavens are overcast. Let us find perfection in each other's flaws. I will compare your bruises to
the galaxy and you can draw flowers on the insides of my
thighs and then pick apart the petals between breathy sighs.
Won't you find signs on my skin that convince you of God's
existence? Won't you find beauty in my body's resistance to
this earth's toil? Won't you lie next to me six feet under the
soil? Is this not true love? Death cannot do us part because
death is only the start of something very new. Hold my hand
dear man—I want to go to Heaven, only with you.

// "a vow"

They ask me who I write about and I tell them it's you. They don't know what you do to me. They don't know how my name sounds so sweet slipping off of your tongue—how it doesn't sound like you've said it, but rather, it was sung. They don't know what it means when you give me that look, like you've opened me up and read all the pages, like I'm only a book. But have you told them the way you've folded my corners and underlined your favorite sentences? Have you told them that you marked the margins with your pen, and filled my pages with your lascivious scent? Have you told them how you've tucked me on the bookshelf countless times, but have come back again and again just to pick me up, climb into bed and read me again? Have you told them how you've memorized my page numbers and all the creases of my spine? Have you told them that you are only mine? Have you told them that this book has only one reader, and the pages would rip themselves out if he ever left her? Have you?

// "won't you read me over and over again?"

You are the sun,
and I am a planet—
always in orbit.
You are the center
of my wonderful
world, and I circle
around you,
gravitated towards
your glowing soul.

// "you are light"

Starving for a lust
close to my skin,
hungry for a pain
to penetrate my veins.
Aching for a touch
soft, gentle, and pure.
Yearning for mystery,
intrigue, and allure.
Your body is sweet,
agile, and lithe.
Your heart beats
along to mine, a
lovely harmony.
Sunlight kisses your
cheeks every morning.
Silhouettes of passion
stain your back.
Your tongue dances
to my swinging
hips and I wonder
when you'll ask
my mouth to
sing along.

// "you are music and song—won't you ask me to dance
along?"

My gums bleed,
flowing between my teeth,
I am choking
on your name,
for the hundredth time
this week,
and I am growing weak
from this love.
Look at what
you have done to me!

// "these memories make me weep"

So often it is the illusion which we wish was true, but our lives are twisted lies and there is no way that I can come back to you. It is half-truths that built up our reality, and there is no way to survive this utter brutality. Finding solace in your arms, is the only escape I know. And with your eyes locked on mine, I can feel our love shine and glow. Take me back to the days when our love was strong and there were no boundaries between right and wrong. I miss the way your fingers traced my lips, just moments before you enveloped me in a maddeningly sweet kiss. How I wish that that reality was solid and absolute, but it seems that my life is an absolute brute. Cruel and savage, it tears apart my dreams—illusions are illusions after all, and they are never what they seem.

// "sometimes i miss the past"

I left my heart in your bed,
under the pillow,
near your head.
I will never forget
what you said that night—
That you would rather
see the light than
see me be right.
I guess that's all right.
Your kisses feel like
cigarette burns on
my skin and before
you think of
"fifty shades of grey,"
let me say that
you are not worth
my time of day.
This piece makes
no sense, but my pen
still flies across
this notebook sheet.
I wish I could fly as quickly
as this beneath
our bed sheets.

// "wants & cravings"

I have swam
through oceans
of thoughts
and drowned
choking on
your name.
The depths of
darkness
always engulfed me
with tired, heavy
loneliness.

// "loneliness is burdensome"

I. I wait for words to illuminate my mind, just as you came and illuminated my life, filling the void with incandescent light. My spine was severed because I craned my neck too hard and too quickly, just to catch a glimpse of your brightness. I was blinded by your purity and beauty—how your gaze caught mine and wandered right into me. You are the man I should have run away from, but I am a flower needing to bloom under the soft heat of your rays and I am rooted in place—in the dirt, is where I will stay. I will grow, reaching towards your heavenly light, hoping that I can finally soak in your essence.

II. Voices are drowned out as I stand here with you, trying to capture the magnificence of your existence—how time runs away from you, hoping to escape those everlasting eyes that hide every secret of the soul. Your gaze holds mine, it seeming like eternity, as I fall headfirst into the pools of whispered darkness that only magnify your dark aura—only, I see incandescent light.

III. Ethereal angels with cascading breaths of diamonds and gems, rise above the darkness with luminous shine, their wings stark pearls against the black of the night.

// "are you not an angel?"

My hands ache from trying
to scrub you off of my
skin,
but your fingerprints still
stain me black.
My eyes hurt from crying
oceans into lands
that would rather
dry out than to
flood its streets
with my pain.
My heart weighs heavy
from
filling its spaces with
your poison, and lust
that was better
left in the dirt.
My head can no
longer contain
thoughts of you, so
I beat it against
the ground,
praying to God
that I'll knock
your branded face

out of my mind.
Your scent still
lingers in my nose,
so I pummel my flesh
bloody and raw
just to escape
memories of you.
I drank venom
off your lips,
thirsty for toxic
desires, but I
can no longer
stomach them.
My feet swell
from running
back and forth,
towards you,
then God,
then back to you,
because there was no way
I could find myself
holding onto both
at once.

// "my mind's continuous war"

I'm romanticizing, fantasizing about your laugh and smile, teeth shining in the bright moonlight as you wrap yourself around my flighty body like a cocoon. It's too soon for you to hear my sighs of aching and wanting and craving, but they will come. Some of my skin tingles from where you have touched it and the rest is aflame from your kisses that trail blissful sighs down the line of my spine. Caress my ribs with your fingers and cup my shoulders in your palms. You have me the way you want me—I am long gone. What is the world when I am lost in ardor and passion? Where my skin is ablaze with an armor of flames that give me no protection from you and your powerful hands? Oh, where did you come from, you ethereal, angelic, and beautiful man?

// "are you not an angel, pt. ii"

I dreamt of my bulging belly and a grin on your face. I swear it's like your smile was the world's only God-given grace. Curly black-haired cherubs with big brown eyes, sleep in their cocoons with soft little sighs. White sheets, intertwined feet, all I could hear was sweet laughter from beneath the blanket. You held my fingers to your black curls, breathing in my scent. I was hell-bent on keeping you mine forever, knowing our days would only be good if we were together. Roses bloomed inside of my heart, filling all the spaces with light and art, pricking away my doubts with thorns that armed me for a battle that was all too worn. You nipped at my ear and I succumbed to your touch, my hands gripped you tight, clutching your sides with dear life. Your breath at my ribs, gave life to my garden.

// "you are my dream"

I look to
the future,
to clumsy kisses
and teeth
knocking into
each other,
just like I
knocked right
into your life—
just like you
knocked the
breath out of me,
when you tripped
into mine.

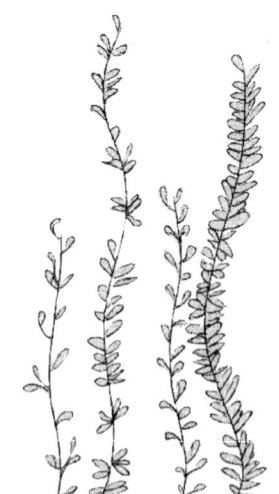

// "was it coincidence or destiny?"

Collide into me,
like our atoms
have collided
and combined
into molecules
of perfection
and utter beauty.
Don't you see
all this chemistry?
I ask myself
what you have
done to me.
You've shared
your strength
in my time of
weakness.
We are now
forever bonded.

// "our chemistry"

Trace the hollows of my bones with your kisses and I will follow with hisses of sighs that slip out from between my teeth as my toes curl with ecstasy. I surrender to you with love and want. I place my hands on your stomach as you stand above me and see your face light up with elation. God blessed me enough to grant me such a wonderful creation that I can call my own. My heart breaks, aching to be held gently in your arms.

// "you are only a fantasy"

You chased sunrays on my chest with your lips and tangled your fingers in my hair while we kissed and covered my wide grin with a fistful of knuckles rubbing my chin and I cried with love and wept with want. You chased after dusk while we lay in the grass basking in twilight because the day flew past us and we only loved in the night when the moon looked down on our tangled frames and as we gasped for air in the silence of the darkness, my heart erupted in flames. You fueled this fire and gave it your name, masking our shame with exclamations of desire—a tauntingly tempting game. I am yours and you are mine, and we will light this fire of love until the end of time. Pyromania isn't a crime, but it does mess with my mind and I am finding that only fire can cure these signs of mental decline. You are my fire. You are the flame. With love in my hand and you in my soul, I can never be tamed.

// "fire cannot be tamed"

I dreamt of all my past demons,
together last night.
I woke in the darkness,
with a terrible fright.
Around me, my demons
lay together in bed.
I yelled out in fear,
for I thought they were dead.
I turned on the lamp
so I could more clearly see,
my demons were in a circle,
all grinning at me.
I flinched in shock,
and drew back in despise,
as my demons turned into you
right before my eyes.

// "you are a haunting demon"

My throat burned with acid reflux, because an influx of emotions rose up through my esophagus from the pit of my stomach and it scorched my lungs along the way. I got bronchitis, wheezing with hardship, and your name echoes with every breath I take and I can't even properly respire for God's sake, but my body chants your name and it's beginning to make me ill.

My head is swimming with thoughts of your love strictly reserved for me and the ache is beginning to pound above my left eye and the light around me is shining too bright, and it glows even when I've closed my eyes. You've made me dizzy with memories and I'm drowning with nausea in my own blood—in my own sickness, I will fade. Here's to the future, where your venom no longer poisons my veins.

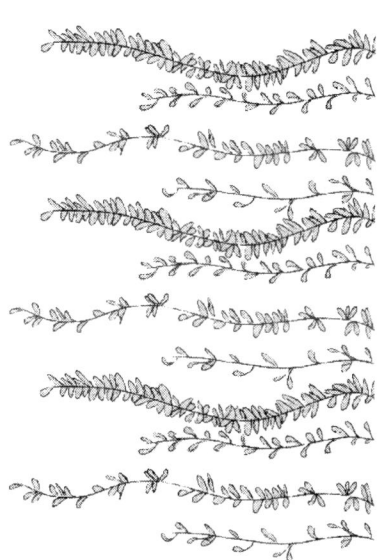

// "your love was poison & i should have known"

I'm exhausted from loving unworthy souls and spilling my heart out just to have my own soul sold. I wrote letters with my blood, but the ink always fades. My thoughts race around and around in circles, but they never really stay. I'm drowning in tiredness—can you see the galaxies under my eyes? Can you tell me what love is, for I can never unveil its disguise? I stared at my reflection until purple spots flashed in the midst of my vision and when I opened my eyes after the dizzying spell passed, I was crushed in a violent collision. I suffered whiplash from wild thoughts and my mouth was blue with wordy bruises, and though I tried to put the blame on myself, I only came up with useless excuses."

// "i am tired, can't you tell?"

Run fast, towards me
I am waiting with arms wide.
Find your home in me

// "for bae"

The way these tights hug my legs make me wish you were wrapped around my limbs keeping them warm and secure in these times of blood and pain. It seems that it is especially during these times that the blood in my veins sings only your name and my heart beats only to your name and my breath escapes only with your name. Your name is on my lips and it is in my heart and it is in my blood. I shed parts of you every month just as I shed my sins and just as I shed my skin.

// "these monthly woes"

I am deliriously close to deteriorating from the inside of my mind. These memories and fantasies make me curl my toes with delight. My breath catches as the sight of your full lips fill my thoughts and your teeth flirtatiously nip my shoulder, taunting me—making me wish we were older. You love the way I close my eyes halfway, the whites still showing. I look half-mad but I am growing wholly mad and in love with you. Your hands at my curves caressing my skin igniting every single nerve within. You strum me like a guitar. Twiddle the strings with your fingers, and I will sigh with every touch of yours that lingers. I sigh deeply, my blood singing your name waiting until I am in your arms again.

// "my blood sings for you"

Your face creeps into my mind,
behind my tired and thoughtful eyes.
I scrutinize this hallucination
with the utmost desire.
My breath catches in my throat
and I find myself entirely undone,
just by thoughts of you
and your sultry stare.
Send upon me more
dreams of sweet, sweet
sin, and I will get
lost in these sensual
visions of skin under
skin.

// "i dream of sin"

I've licked your
salted wounds with
aching, devil lips
and have danced
        on the graves of
        our dying love.
      I am free of
        such shackles
          and am free
        of such burdens
        yet my heart
      still claims
      to feel heavy.

// "our love is dead"

You can count the stars in the sky, and I will count the ridges in your spine and we will redefine the idea of passion that should exist in our veins. The kind that keeps us wholly sane when it rains and it pours and our sorrows drown our lungs with blood, flooding the space in our hearts with memories and dust, clouding our mind with the lust that once was. Just keep counting the stars and I'll keep counting these ridges and we will bridge hearts together, stamping love in their minds, a kind that can last forever. You and I will be always and forever.

// "hopeless romance"

Lipstick stains pain my brain when I think of abstaining from staining your veins with my venom. You have bruised my lips with your kisses and my skin has turned to amethyst and ebony. This ecstasy is not enough for me and I need more of you in my blood, so poison me like I have poisoned you, and turn my purpling lips to dark blue.

// "your love marked my skin"

I am captured, enraptured by your soul, caught in the tangled web of your essence. I am sensing love build up inside of me, blooming like a flower of great beauty and of great life. I sacrificed the earth and my roots, for I know that you will rip me out of the dirt one day and claim me as yours. You will water my leaves and grant me hours of sunlight, but my roots will dry when you forget. And you will forget. My petals will shrivel up and die, just because you forgot to tell me you love me, just one time, and it will all disappear, in just a blink of an eye. My stem will bend and it will break at your touch and I will be broken forevermore. When you toss me back into the dirt without shedding even one teardrop, I will finally find quiet peace once again with the earth.

// "i am a flower"

We thought our love
was an endless,
torrential waterfall,
like this rain,
but slowly and
surely,
we stopped pouring;
there wasn't a
drop left at all.

// "our love was only a chapter"

Sometimes I am overwhelmed with how much I love him / and then I am overwhelmed because God gave me a chance to save my soul and let me turn back to Him / and when I turned back to my Lord, he granted me mercy / and with that mercy I was granted ease / who knew that life would be so easy and content / I contend that I should have turned to Him long ago / but it's better to come back than never to come at all / I come to you with open palms raised towards the sky / grant me a man of yours, my Lord, make him mine for the rest of our lives / write his name next to mine / write our happiness in children counting any from one to five / write for us an adopted child or two so we can fill his life with smiles / write for us paradise, write for us to be together / write for our love to grow / write for our parents and children, rewards and more / forgive us for our sins, my Lord, grant us your shade / seal our love for You in each other on that day our marriage is made / put in our hearts faith stronger than any adversity / and keep us safe and secure, shrouded in your mercy / make us of the righteous, the pious, and proud / make us of those whose shining faces bright with noor stand out in the crowd / I beg of you my Lord, make us of your favorite slaves / I pray in my heart that he and I will be amongst the saved.

// "a vow, pt. ii"

I.   I licked sweat off your skin and you kissed the sin off of mine and we swore to each other that we'd survive until the very end of time. But the clock was ticking and we were running out of hours so we plucked stars from the sky and had them devoured. Fire burned in our chests and we called it passion, but wearing sins on our sleeves was a short-lived fashion. And my knees were weak and so was my heart but I didn't think that I could ever have the strength to pull apart. Your lips branded my skin black, just like they branded my soul, and something under my nose always smelled foul but I overlooked the pain and overlooked the guilt in the hopes that denial would keep these blooms alive before they started to wilt.

II.   The flowers were dying and I was losing myself too, but just when I thought I was gaining some strength, I made the mistake of looking at you. Your eyes were glowing bright with tears and your lips quivered with surprise, and suddenly I could not fathom why I would have given up such a prize.

III.   When your eyes flashed with menace and from your tongue, slipped threats, I knew that I had gone way in over my head. With fervor in my heart and a desire to walk the straight path, I paid no mind to empty promises of incurring your wrath. I turned to my Lord, with heaviness in my bones and with a stroke of a pen, He wrote freedom upon my stone. Sunrise dawned throwing shadows in my wake, but I was not scared, for now I was in God's shade.

// "god gave me another chance"

My eyes
have bled
from imprints
of grotesque
love, branded
behind these eyelids.
I wonder if they
think this love
is true.

// "real love is kind"

The chill
is beginning
to diminish,
but my bones
still weigh
heavy
from memories—
from you.
Your face
is blurry behind
my eyelids,
and your name
no longer
burns my tongue.
Strange,
that I cannot
even recall
who you are.

// "it is strange to be strangers"

Darling, you are a work of art. From that angled and royal nose, to that strong and willful heart. I knew that it was love that pulled me to you from the very start. God took His time in carving you out. Of your beauty and soul, I have no doubt. Your face shines with the light of a thousand moons; so mysterious, thoughtful, and unreachable—like for a moon that a lone wolf wistfully croons. You are a masterpiece, my love, perfection at its peak. Just the thought of you actually being mine makes my knees go weak.

// "i will take you to museums and leave you hanging there"

I want to
drown in the
storms of
your tears
and hurricanes
of your sadness.
I want to
dance in the

tornadoes
of your anger
and stumble
upon the
quaking earth
when you are
filled with rage.
I want to be
engulfed
by the tsunamis
of your love

and burn
with passion
when volcanoes
erupt with
your joy.

// "i want you entirely"

I'm still trying
to erase
the remnants
of your touch
off of my
heart and off
of my skin,
but the black
stains still
remain—
they brand
me as a
sinner.

// "will i ever forgive myself?"

You are better
than your sins,
better than your
weakening heart,
and far better
than the past that
always weighed you
down with
shame.

// "note to self"

And now we part ways.
Thank you for
journeying along
with me.
I ask you to
forgive yourself
and love yourself
and remember that
you are stronger
than you know.
Your burdens are
great, but your
heart is even
greater.
You were born
with greatness.
Never forget.

// "dear reader"

Acknowledgments Pt. I

God
For His infinite mercy and blessings.

<u>Mama & Baaba</u>
Thank you both for being my #1 fans. Your encouragement and support have been the backbone of who I am and what I have achieved. I cannot say thank you enough, but I will spend the rest of my life trying anyway. Thank you for your honesty and your advice, your love and your kindness, your understanding and your mercy. You are forever the loves of my life and the light of my eyes.

| HH | SS | | NZ | SA |
f.b.a. / h.s. / s.a.

Acknowledgement Pt. II

To the many souls that have lent me their light, their
flames, their fire.
To the women who have survived, despite their
cracked bones.
To those whose souls weigh heavy with secrets and
sins—do not let your past cast shadows on your
path. Light the way with forgiveness and wisdom.

Thank you to my mentors and teachers who never
ceased to give me their encouragements and advice.

A special thank you to the following poets for giving
me the courage to not only continue writing, but to
share it with the world.
Your words are great. Your hearts are greater.

| Naveed Khan
| Key "Asiya" Ballah

About the Illustrator

Jolene Sadoun has nurtured a love for art since her first illustrating class at the Columbus College of Art and Design at the age of six. She has a strong affinity towards all that is dark and mysterious and presents those concepts throughout her artwork. The illustrations introduced in these pages explore thematic elements inspired by Huda Bint Adnan's work, which examine the journey of finding redemption from God and forgiveness from oneself.

Though Jolene's veins flow with watercolor paint (and coffee), she utilizes several art forms ranging from watercolor painting, monochromatic sketching, and pointillism. Jolene has also successfully dabbled with poetry and Photoshop, of which the results can be seen on her social media. Jolene's goal is to use art in its various forms to make a positive impact on a person's life and, even if one person is moved by something she has created, she will have achieved her goal.

Jolene, originally from Ohio, currently studies Psychology at the University of Houston. As a part-time fairy, she takes part in many volunteer efforts, illustrates as self-therapy, and holds an interest in social activism.

Contact: ineedasandwich@yahoo.com

About the Author

By: Mohammad Mitha

I present to you, dear reader, your author. She reins from the city of Calcutta in the eastern outskirts of India, but grew up in suburbia Houston where she studies Education at the University of Houston. But do not be mistaken, for Huda Bint Adnan is no tourist in the world of emotion. Her poetry bleeds the words of a soul who has travelled far across the globe, experienced much pain and suffering, and dared greatly to become something of herself. With each struggle life has thrown at her, she has endured. With each passing moment, she is a living embodiment that one can not only tame their demons, but can stand upon their shoulders and call out, "I am greater."

Each poem is cathartic in nature, yet simple in complexity. Each poem screams of emotion, yet remains subtle in its presentation. Huda has mastered the fine art of conveying her emotions in a manner succinct and in a presentation minimal. With each line read, we feel as if she's lived amongst us. With each line read, we hear our hearts whisper, "I have felt so, too." On reaching the end, we lean back as our souls let out a soft, barely audible gasp, "Truer words were never spoken."

I've only just acquainted myself with Huda Adnan (and barely, at that). But the truth is, her poetry speaks to me as if I've known her my whole life. As if she's known *me* her whole life. Perhaps you'll find an old friend within these pages. Perhaps you'll find yourself; the words you've always wanted to voice, but were unable to form between your lips. Perhaps you'll find yourself falling in love with her writing, just as I did. But perhaps, most importantly, you may find your soul released from its shackles, set free by Huda's vindicating and alleviating words, written in the language only heartbreak can understand, and lived by one who has come to understand them all.

Contact: hudita27@gmail.com

Made in the USA
Lexington, KY
30 October 2019